How Women Use Their Inner Wisdom

Intuitive Training for Finding True Love

RUTH BERGER

BALBOA.
PRESS

A DIVISION OF HAY HOUSE

Balboa Press books may be ordered through booksellers or by contacting:

Balboa Press
A Division of Hay House
1663 Liberty Drive
Bloomington, IN 47403
www.balboapress.com
1 (877) 407-4847

Printed in the United States of America.

ISBN: 978-1-4525-9243-5 (sc)
ISBN: 978-1-4525-9245-9 (hc)
ISBN: 978-1-4525-9244-2 (e)

Library of Congress Control Number: 2014902603

Balboa Press rev. date: 3/27/2014

To the most important people in my life:

My husband Dan, who never ceases to give me unconditional love, and take care of my every need.

MY first born daughter Karri, a psychiatric nurse who helps people who suffer from physical and emotional problems. She is a advocate for individuals who require explanations on why the doctor needs you to take a medical test, medicines, etc. She's like the go-between the medical world and the patient.

My youngest daughter Penny, is an amazing totally blind woman who uses her inner power to see more than most people with 20-20 vision. She can give you an perfect ID about your loved one in spirit and relate a messages to you from them.

These three individuals make my life a joy. I love them very much and grateful for their love and friendship.

"To effectively communicate, we must realize that we are all different in the way we perceive the world and use this understanding as a guide to our communication with others."

----- Tony Robbins

"Beginning today, treat everyone you meet as if they were going to be dead by midnight. Extend to them all the care, kindness, and understanding you can muster, and do it with no thought of any reward. Your life will never be the same again."

----- Og Mansion

Some of the names and descriptions in this book have been changed to protect people's privacy.

Contents

Introduction

Dear Reader,

I believe that everyone can find True Love naturally or by using How Women Use Their Inner Power to find perfect partners.

Years ago I read a book about two earths. One that was in present time, where the other earth, was a place where individuals could replay their lives the way they wished they had.

In my over forty years of giving workshops and readings to thousands of people, I hear three questions often about love, health, and finances, love being the most asked.

When people don't love themselves, they can't understand how to love anyone else.

I wrote *How Women Use Their Inner Power,* to teach people how to trust their intuition to have healthier relationships. It is my wish that we could have a happier world and everyone could understand how to find their true loves.

I welcome your comments.

With much love and blessings,
Ruth Berger

Chapter 1

How Women Use Their Inner Power

I remember watching my daughter Karri, combing and twirling my mother's thick, wavy, dark hair for hours, like she was playing with a doll.

My mother was dying of Cancer and in a lot of pain. Karri just wanted her to feel better, and so she combed, curled and applied cream all over her face, telling her how lovely she looked.

My mother would smile and fall asleep.

Karri knew how to use her inner power a lot in those days. She was a natural healer.

She never tired of treating my mother in a kind and loving manner. She had a special way of caring and loving others. Her love of animals was amazing.

I was afraid of animals, and was in awe of Karri's animal love.

Karri was so different than me. She loved critters of all types; cats, dogs, birds, and even rats.

As a small child I lived in a rat infested neighborhood, and often saw king size rats roaming the alley behind our home, trying to eat the cat food our next-door neighbor put out in a dish for his cat. But the rats always got there first. I was grateful they didn't try to eat me.

Then one night I woke up to see a king rat, as big as any cat I'd ever seen, staring at me from the doorway to my bedroom. I screamed and my parents came running.

Afterwards I dreamt often about that rat so close, staring at me.

My mother told me about the time my face was licked by a wild dog in my buggy outside our front door. I got sick, and my parents had to get a 24-hour nurse for three days to give me tender loving care. I don't remember the incident, but afterwards I avoided all dogs.

Karri got sick a lot. I used my inner power to know when to take her to a doctor.

Soon after her father brought home a squirrel monkey, without asking me. Within two days, Karri began having 103-104 temperatures almost immediately.

When I asked the doctor, "does she have an allergy to the monkey?"

He said, "Does she touch the monkey?"

"No," I said.

"Then I don't see how she could be allergic to the monkey," he answered.

I married David, my first husband and the father of Karri, who was also an animal lover, but totally insensitive to my fears of animals. He often told other people that he traded his horse for me. I didn't like that comparison and thought he was thoughtless and unkind.

I began to be more observant of how David played with the monkey and how he never washed his hands before giving Karri a feeding to give me a chance to catch up on my lack of sleep.

I told the doctor how David never washed his hands before giving Karri some milk and once more, I asked, "Could he be passing on the monkey's germs to Karri?

The doctor said, "It's possibility."

That's all I needed to hear. The mother lion in me roared, "Get rid of the monkey of I'll divorce you."

Afraid he returned the monkey to the pet store, Karri's high temperatures lessened.

I envied karri's lack of fear around animals.

Karri was always the caring, loving daughter I ever wanted. She knew how to use her inner power long before I knew what it was.

By the time I was married four years, I'd had three children and my life was busy taking care of the children and my home. MY husband didn't want to help out so he didn't.

Fortunately my mother lived downstairs and was kind enough to give me tips on how to three children. She delivered four sons, I was the only girl.

My mother was an old fashion mom, who cooked hot meals at night, cleaned the house and raised her family well.

My grandmother lived with us, also a special lady, who didn't speak English, but I learned to speak Jewish a little to her. She was kind and compassionate.

One day I ate the chocolate candy on her dresser and got sick. It wasn't candy, it was something to aid the body in releasing foods. I had an horrendous bout of diarrhea and never ate any more of her candy

My mother gave me piano lessons, in spite of my father saying, "Women get married and have children, I'll be wasting spending money on your musical training."

He was wrong. I was the only child who used musical training to help myself heal and teach others how to play the piano. Music gave me a way to relieve my stress.

In four years I delivered two girls and a son. I was a busy mother, and a stay-at-home mom, who also cooked hot meals every night and raised my children. I was busy, but loving it all.

Only my husband drove me up the walls. He got a terrorizing terrier to keep him company. I was afraid of the dog who kept trying to bite me.

Years late I learned from a famous English psychic, that dogs sensed my fears and didn't understand why I was frightened. It took me many more years to be able to pet a dog.

It was the women in my life who taught me how to use my inner power. Each one in her own way, showed me how to be a better person and mother.

I came home one day from work to hear Penny talking to someone in her bedroom. She was only four.

I quietly went to her room and saw my mother's ghost lying next to her in bed.

Horrified I'd had always been taught that when people die, they don't return. I didn't want my daughter doing something that might hurt her. I yelled, "Don't talk to ghosts any more."

As I left her room I heard her quietly say, "Shhh!. We have to talk quieter. My mommy's afraid."

Penny wasn't afraid, but I was.

Karri wasn't afraid of animals but I was. I thought this isn't right. I need to stop being afraid, but wasn't sure how to rid my fears.

That's when I began to pray daily to God to give me courage to fight my fears.

The next few years were filled with happy children and playing my piano, which I loved more each day.

Then one day, my brother Paul, the only redhead in the family and two years older than me, was studying to be a medical doctor said, "Ruth if you want to play in the high school orchestra, you'll need to be a better accompanist. I will teach you."

I nodded yes because I realized he understood how much this meant to me.

When Karri was fourteen, her father asked me for a divorce. I was happy. He told me how lousy a wife I was, and then preceded to blast me for things I'd never done to all our friends. He omitted telling them about building a canoe in our kitchen, that I had to walk around, over and under to cook and serve our children.

After six months, he had to cut the boat in half to get it out of our house. I would have it cut free months earlier.

I was glad to be free of him.

His girlfriend was only three-years-older than Karri, not even eighteen. She had been working as a prostitute, in the hotel where David worked. They were well suited for each other.

The night I returned from the divorce court, and walked into my apartment, listening to the quiet peace. I realized I'd never have to listen to David's complaints again. I felt freer than ever before in my life.

My prayers had been answered

Ruth Berger

Thank you Penny, for showing me that being blind is not the end, but the beginning of seeing more than most people with 20/20 vision. Her enthusiasm is contagious and I am grateful that she is in my life.

The Beginning

**How Women Use Their Inner Power,
Chapter 1.**

Inner Power is the combination of creative thinking, intelligence, past experiences, and faith.

"Affirming daily that only good will come to you, is a great way to begin your day."

After my mother had three sons before me, I prayed she'd have a girl the next time she got pregnant. I wanted a sister to sleep with in my bedroom, to talk to, and share things girls talked about.

Instead I got another brother. Growing up as the only girl of four brothers, I wanted to have the same freedom as they did, but my mother wanted me to be behave like a girl.

I loved to play baseball. I ran fast, and could catch the balls that were hit high and far. But the boys never picked me to be on their side.

Growing up was hard being the only girl and the smallest in my family.

My father decided his children should become a musical team to play for special events. He gave each of my four brothers a musical instrument, and paid for their lessons and music.

Aaron was given a violin, Henry a cello, and Paul, got a clarinet and saxophone. Joe was the comedian. He played at the piano.

Ruth Berger

My father refused to pay for my music lessons as he thought girls only grew up to be mothers and wives; He thought I would never use my music to earn a living, and it would be a waste of his money.

Fortunately my mother paid for my lessons and music out of her food allowance.

Chapter 2

How Men Use Their Inner Power

I was walking to the orchestra room on the fourth floor of my high school to practice the piano, when I met two girls oohing and aahing about a boy, who was handsome that played the violin like a virtuoso.

They were talking about my brother Aaron, who had an uncanny ability to add up rows of figures to the total number and be correct. He would just run his fingers alongside of the numbers and then say the total. He was always right.

Aaron was handsome, smart and a great brother.

Henry, the second oldest brother, played the cello in the orchestra. He liked to hit me, but was always teaching me how to defend myself with others.

One day he tried to surprise me by saying boo as I walked into a room. Suddenly I remembered what he taught me and flipped him over my head about six feet away.

Stunned, he never surprised me again.

My brother Paul said, "Ruth if you want to play in the high school orchestra you'll need to be a better accompanist. I will teach you.

He knew how to help me.

He said, "When I play my saxophone, listen and stop when I stop."

When I did so, he said, "Now when I pause, you pause, even if the music has been written differently."

We did this for a few weeks until I got good at it.

When I tried out for the orchestra I was accepted immediately, and in addition, was asked to be the accompanist for the Boy's Chorus and for special events. I was excited about these unexpected requests. Joy filled my body with yellow (happy) energy.

Joe, my youngest brother was the comedian of the family. He played at the piano. He was funny.

High school opened me up to a different life. I could stay out longer, have more friends and play the piano for the orchestra, the boy's chorus and special events. I loved my life and wanted more. I was a good student.

Playing the piano stopped many of my fears.

The first day playing for the Boys Chorus reunited me with David, a young man from my grammar school days. He invited me to go see his horse. I didn't like horses, but I went anyway.

At the stable where his horse was boarded, he rode the horse while I went inside the barn and read a book. David was tall, good looking and had a great smile, but I still didn't like him.

I liked Chuck, another violinist boy in my class, who wasn't born in my faith.

When my mother met David and found out he was Jewish, she was overjoyed. I wasn't. She kept pushing me to marry David so I wouldn't become an old maid. I was only eighteen.

Use your Inner Power to
Trust your instincts Naturally.

My father asked me to come to his men's clothing store to watch for thieves. He set a folding table outside in front of his men's clothing store, with piles of men's slacks on top.

I looked and watched for thieves but wasn't sure what they looked like, until I saw an elderly man getting fat as he touched a pile of slacks.

I told my four brothers about him and they immediately surrounded the man and discovered he was hiding pants under his long coat.

I became a hero overnight in my family.

Gypsies lived next door to my dad's shop. The women wore satin low cut blouses and no underwear. They wore them to deliberately distract the men while other gypsies stole their money and other valuables.

One of the gypsy women often pinched her child's rump whenever a tourist walked by.

When the child screamed, the gypsy would hold out her hand and say, "She is hungry and we have no money to buy food."

The tourist would pull out a $5 or $10 bill and give it to the gypsy.

I vowed never to lie or harm another person

Everywhere I went, strangers would tell me intimate stories about their lives. I loved listening to them.

In numerology I learned that the number one represented independence, wanting to work alone. But when I accompanied another person, either in speech or music, we formed a twosome, which meant we were co-creating. I liked co-creating.

I married David at nineteen and had my first child before I was twenty-one.

My child Karri was born with a cleft pallet, which made her unable to drink or eat normally. It often took two hours to get her to drink one ounce of milk.

David was not a good provider. He couldn't keep a job. He always blamed his bosses, but he was not a good employee. Always complaining.

I needed more money and didn't have many ways to earn more.

Lonely, I attended a Tupperware Party and heard the speaker talk about how easy it was to earn money as a Tupperware dealer.

"You only have to hire a baby sitter when you need one. The rest of the week you are free to take care of your home and children."

That sounded good, so I learned how to be a Tupperware dealer. The first assignment was to book five Tupperware parties.

David said, "You can't even talk in front of two people. And we don't have the money for you to buy a starter kit." I lost my confidence but our need for money kept me going.

I didn't want to ask my friends or relatives to give me a party, so I started knocking on doors with my children. Nothing happened until Penny kept saying, "Mommy I have to go to the bathroom."

The woman said, "She can use our bathroom." Finally a yes!

We talked for a few minutes and I told her I had just become a Tupperware dealer and how hard it was to get my first five shows.

She smiled and looking down at Penny she said, "I'll be your first show."

Two years later I worked hard and became one of the top 25 dealers and in the top 20 managers in the country. I liked people and they liked me. And that was only the beginning of my public speaking career and the ability to let go of some of my fears.

Chapter 3

Medical Intuition

David took over Karri's 2am feeding so I could get some sleep. A few days later, he brought home a pet squirrel monkey as a surprise to me. He forgot to ask if I wanted a monkey, which of course I didn't.

The next day Karri began getting temperatures of 102/103 degrees. I called the doctor to make a house call and asked, "Could she be allergic to the monkey?"

"Does she touch the monkey?" He said.

"No."

"Then I don't think it's the monkey giving her the higher temps."

My mind kept saying, Karri is allergic to the monkey. A mother's hunch, but the doctor kept saying no.

I kept thinking why does she get the temps in the afternoon, and not at any other time of day or night. What was different at that hour?"

I just knew David was the reason. Over and over I pondered until I realized David never washed his hands before handling our baby, and he was wearing the pajamas he wore when he played with the monkey. That's got to be it.

I told the doctor and he said, "Maybe!"

That's all I needed to hear. I told David in my mother lion voice, "You either get rid of the monkey or I'm leaving you."

He didn't want to give up the monkey, but my daughter was being harmed. He returned the monkey, and Karri's temperature returned to normal.

During the next three years I had a hysterectomy and got a divorce from David. For the first time, I was free at last. Ah! Life was good

Hunches are intuitive feelings, which come from the same place as imagination.

Have you ever had a hunch and didn't listen?

Did you wish you had heeded your instincts?

A man, trying to steal clothes, has just shot Morris Krichevsky, owner of Morris and Sons, in his men's clothing store.

Horrified I heard the radio broadcaster talking about my father. "Morris is in critical condition and is on his way to the hospital."

I almost hit another car as I pulled over to the side of the road to hear the details. I knew the hospital he was being taken to and drove directly there.

My brother Aaron was waiting for me. He put his arms around me and said, " Our mother saw the robber shoot our dad. I looked at my mother, who was ghastly white; I thought she'd faint.

We hugged and cried.

At that point, a doctor came out and said, "Morris has to have immediate surgery. Sit down and get comfortable. You're going to have a long wait."

Six hours later the doctor returned and said, 'Morris had a heart attack and we had to stop. He'll have to come for more surgery when he's better. He's in good shape for a man of seventy-two years."

We were so relieved, we all laughed. My father had been a health nut for years. He fasted one day a week to give his body a rest. Every day he would put his hands on the floor and walk like a gorilla back and forth. That was his way of keeping fit. Obviously it worked. He lived another thirty years to be one-hundred-years-old plus three days.

Six weeks later he had his second surgery and began to improve.

Two months later, my father walked five miles to see his optometrist. The doctor couldn't believe Morris had walked that far. By this time many people had heard about my father being shot in a holdup.

I learned a valuable lesson from my dad that day he walked through the heaviest snow Chicago had ever seen, to the doctor for his eye exam.

"Why did you walk in all that snow? Don't you know you could have died from a heart attack?"

He said, "The doctor said I have a heart condition. I didn't believe him"

My dad taught me how to be a positive thinker.

Years later a doctor told me, "You have emphysema and it cannot be cured."

I couldn't understand how I could get a smoker's condition when I'd never smoked. In those days, second hand smoke was not believed to contribute to lung problems.

The doctor didn't believe I'd never smoke.

I knew he was wrong and thought about my dad's words about his heart forecast. Everything in me was yelling, "Don't believe his diagnosis."

I heard in my head. "You will be well."

Six years later, after a strict diet of Basmati rice three times a day for eighteen months, and breathing exercises, I gave away my three oxygen tanks and started breathing normally.

I was cured!

"You are essentially who you create yourself to be and all that occurs in your life is the result of your own making."

— **<u>Stephen Richards</u>,**
<u>Think Your way to Success;</u>
<u>Let Your Dreams Run</u>

Shortly after my lungs healed, a friend called to tell me about an ad she read in the newspaper about an upcoming week of healing and intuitive training. She suggested I call Paul Johnson, the name in the ad, and ask where the conference was to be held and who could come.

I had a high temperature and could hardly speak, but she insisted I call. Something inside told me to do it."

When I spoke to Paul Johnson, he said, "You should come in for a healing right away."

I asked, "Are you a doctor?"

He said, ""No. But I can help you get well."

I'd never heard about a hands-on-healing, so I brought my daughter Penny with me for a back healing. I watched as Paul put his hands on her back and saw her body light up as if a bulb was lit.

She looked happier and when she got off his table, she said, "I feel better."

Now I was ready for Paul to put his hands on me. The first thing he did was hold his hands about five inches away from my chest.

I began to feel heat and opened my eyes to see if he had put a heat lamp over me. He hadn't.

I began to feel more heat and felt my body getting electrical surges of energy. I didn't understand why I was having these feelings but my body felt better.

My head stopped hurting and suddenly I could speak in a normal voice without croaking.

"What did you do?" I asked Paul.

He said, "I mentally sent healing energy into your lungs."

Bewildered, "I asked, "How did you do that?"

He said, "Come to my healing conference next week, and you'll learn how to do what I do."

"Is that possible?" Paul nodded yes and smiled. He helped me get off the table that he had asked me lie on.

I went home and took my temperature. It was 98.6, normal. I couldn't believe that someone's hands could help me heal without medicine.

This was the beginning of another new turn in my life.

Believing in the unknown!

Seeing is Believing

Chapter 4

What Color is My Aura?

The first morning of Paul Johnson's healing training week, he instructed everyone to hold hands while inhaling and exhaling, and singing, "I love you and you love me. We're a happy family."

My body got hot from this exchange. As time moved on I got so hot, I thought I'd burn up.

Taking extra sensory training helped my inner power to think above my fears. I knew I had found my life's path.

Shortly after, a friend asked, "Ruth, can you give a short ESP demonstration for our charity group?"

I had been thinking of speaking before small groups.

The law of attraction, which I learned about at the healing conference certainly works fast, I thought.

I wasn't sure how to do it, but she was persistent.

To my surprise, I answered yes while my body kept saying no.

The evening came and I arrived at the meeting place. There were eighty people waiting for me. Terror struck. Why had I said yes?

I asked the audience to please make a line and I would answer them personally one at a time.

After giving three more people a mini reading, my friend said, "Everyone wants to hear what you're saying."

I was so stunned. I couldn't say the same things to more then two people. I'd look like a fool. And what if I was wrong? All my fears surfaced.

My friend gave me a thumbs up sign and nodded her head yes, "Go for it Ruth. You'll be great."

I wish I had her optimism.

Forty minutes later I was exhausted and my eyes were burning. I went to the bathroom and noticed my eyes were bloody. "Never again I vowed."

I left the bathroom and saw two women waiting for me. The first woman said, "You were so good. Would you do the same type of show for my charity group?"

Everything in me wanted to shout, No! But my mouth said yes. I wanted to run, and in spite of the way I was thinking, we booked a show a week away.

I said yes to the second lady also, wondering what was wrong with me. Everything in my body was yelling no, and still I said yes.

A year went by and I was up to giving one show a week, always fearing the worst. But I was earning money that we needed and that kept me saying yes.

At the show, I heard a woman announcing, "Ruth Berger is an unusual psychic. She sees more, hears more, knows more, but won't tell you anything until you ask her a question?"

Money kept me doing what I was afraid of. People kept saying how good I was. I found that hard to believe since I could never remember what I said. Fear was holding me captive.

****

I was asked to do my first radio show. I was so terrified that I lost my voice. Fortunately I got it back before the first caller asked a question.

After my first book, *The Secret Is In The Rainbow was published, readers kept asking me, "What Color is my Aura?" which became my most asked question.*

****

"Can you tell me what color my aura is? I just finished reading your book. *And I'm curious if you can see an aura around me."*

I didn't want to tell her that if she didn't have an aura, she wouldn't be alive in twenty-four hours, so I looked at her head and and thankfully was able to say, "The aura on your left side is a light brown, which indicates you've been working on a practical idea, something you've been thinking about for years."

She said, "You're right. I've been writing a book and it's about how to begin a business. What else do you see?"

The aura on your right side is a bright green, so your idea will earn you a lot of money soon.

"Oh thank you," she said. "That's what I was hoping you'd tell me. I have high hopes for this book."

"So do I. It is going to be a best seller!"

A young couple asked, "Our six year-old-son sees auras too.

"Really!" I looked at their son's blue-black hair hiding behind his mother's skirt and asked, "What color is your mother's aura?"

The boy instantly said, "Blue."

I looked at his mother and asked her, "Do you like to learn?"

"Yes," she said. I'm studying how to be a nurse."

"Blue is the color for higher learning. Your son is right. Congratulations!"

Auras are easy to see when you believe you can see them.

I suggest that people close their eyes to shut off any color distractions so they can see with their inner sight.

Many people don't believe they can so they don't see.

****

I always see hazes of colors around people's heads.

When I began giving intuitive private sessions to clients, I would gaze at his/her head to see which side was darkest.

If the left side was darkest, it meant the person was still making bad decisions because of negative past events.

The lighter the color, the better decisions the person would make.

The right side represented the present.

A client asked, "Will I get the new job I applied for?"

Her aura was black and so large, it was overpowering me.

I knew that if I didn't do something immediately I would fall into a lower level of mind power.

I closed my eyes and heard a message from my spirit teachers, "Project sliding glass doors before you, on one side you can see yourself, and on the other side, you can see your future

Then slide the door on the right side (the present) open so your inner power can come through."

I did and immediately saw her dark black aura shrink and her right side aura became light and then yellow."

This is when I began to use my inner power in a more directed fashion.

I was so happy. "Yes, you will get the job if you remember to surround yourself with happy thoughts. Imagine getting the job.

"Wear a medium blue color blouse to accelerate your mind power." Her shoulders relaxed as she accepted my words and two weeks later, she said, "I got the job. Thanks for all your suggestions."

Use your inner power to protect your aura.

Have you ever seen an aura around someone's head?

Many paintings of Jesus show a cloud of light around his head, indicating how spiritual he was. The color on both sides of the head, meant he was fully spiritually developed.

"If you don't see an aura immediately, close your eyes and see with your inner power. Say to yourself, "If I could see the aura, the color would be......."

Keep practicing until you see more.

Watch politicians on television to see their auras clearer. They are usually on display with lights and backgrounds. Watch for dark clouds coming out of their mouths when they talk.

Dark clouds means lying.

****

A friend called sobbing. "I haven't been able to get any information about my fifteen year old daughter who's been missing for two weeks. I've called all her friends and no one seems to know what's happened to her. Can you tune in and tell me where she is?"

Her voice was loud and anxious.

"Calm down while I try to tune into her." Instantly I imagined a white cloud pouring from the sky upon my body to block her fears.

I said, "I don't get any bad feelings about her. She seems confused and almost depressed. I want you to imagine a white cloud hovering over her and believing that she's fine. I see her calling you today."

She calmed down and did what I suggested. Later that day she got a call from an elderly woman, who told her. "We both saw a beautiful teenager stumbling.

They suggested she come home with them for food and rest. She didn't seem to know who she was? The couple was fearful she might be harmed if they didn't do something.

Then two weeks later, the teenager suddenly spoke to the couple and said her name and phone number. Please call my parents and tell them to come and get me. This happened an hour after my friend called me.

Fear prevented the mother from hearing her daughter's cry for help.

Fear doesn't allow you to trust your higher inner power. Love removes the fear. Once they were reunited, the daughter explained that once she had gotten so afraid, she forgot who she was.

Chapter 5

Power Attacks

Have you ever had lunch with a friend and felt totally drained afterwards?

Perhaps she talked about a negative experience she had with someone.

How did you feel?

Were you able to shake off the bad feelings afterwards?

If this happens to you often, it's time to know how to use your inner power to protect you.

****

Are you forever in a rush, staving off exhaustion?

Are you desperately overcommitted, afraid to say NO?

Do you have fang marks from being bled dry by energy vampires?

Does the onslaught of violence in the news leave you drained?

Do you have a keen imagination and vivid dreams?

Is time alone each day as essential to you as food and water?

Are you too shy or too sensitive according to others?

Do noises and confusion quickly overwhelm you?

If you answered yes to most of the questions, you may be an empathic.

Empathic people tend to take on the fears or pains of others, whether they're alive or in the spirit world.

As an empathic person, others are already coming to you for reassurance and a safe place to process their confusion.

You cannot resolve their fears, but what you can do, is go within to a place of constancy, radiance and calm, and bring forth a shield to protect you, while meditating and connecting with your own inner center of strength and calm.

One way to protect your aura is to visualize talking inside a glass telephone booth.

Imagine a white cloud pouring over you with peace and serenity. Take a moment or two to feel the difference.

If you've done it correctly, you'll feel lighter and happier.

Redo the exercise to get a different response.

It's always good to get a second opinion.

In the world today, there are many people afraid of poverty, crime, and negative stories from the media.

It's imperative to keep your aura and sanity safe.

Overly sensitive people will attract the negative energies of others in restaurants, movie theaters, sporting events.

Always be alert if you suddenly get frightened for no reason.

You may be getting a power attack from someone else. Do not push this aside as unimportant. Instead see yourself being covered by a white cloud and see it reducing your negative feelings.

****

One night I woke up seeing two men trying to kill my daughter Penny.

Because I was afraid, I didn't realize I was looking through the wall. I opened my eyes, and looked at the clock. It was 3AM.

"Whom was I picking up? I asked myself and got the name, "Joy." It was too late to call my friend. I calmed myself down and waited till 9AM to call her and ask, "What were you doing this morning at 3AM?"

She said, " I was screaming from a nightmare of two men trying to kill my child."

I had a power attack from a good friend. She wasn't trying to hurt me, just calling for help from me. I'd always been there for her. It was natural for her to want my help.

I told her what I'd dreamt and we comforted each other.

Joy was a dear friend who seemed to be on my psychic hotline.

Tommy was another hotline connection. One day I panicked hearing their names. They had each been at different grocery parking lots when their cars were hit. I felt like I'd had an explosion.

Prayers and thinking positive thoughts calmed me down.

The title of my first book *The Secret Is In The Rainbow was chosen because the lighter colors give the best decisions. I rated the colors from one to 10, one being the lightest and 10, the darkest.*

Watching politicians on television is fun. Their auras were easier to see because they often stand in bright lights with a darker background, for more than a few minutes.

I wanted to see which side of his/her head was darkest.

If the left side was darker it may have been because others may have convinced the politicians that telling a lie would get him elected. The darkness of that side indicated he was making a bad decision.

Then I began to follow the darkness to know why he had to lie. If the dark haze ended at his throat, his ego was overwhelming his common sense. If the dark haze went direct to his heart, he truly was afraid. He needed to use his higher power to make the right decision.

If you can't see an aura, close your eyes to see more without the distraction of other colors.

Chapter 6

Creating a Wonderful Day

Being A Psychic Medium is like riding a different roller coaster every day. I never know what's going to happen.

Upon awakening I ask my inner power,

What wonderful thing will happen to me today?

Perhaps I had been waiting for a test result and possible surgery, which was frightening.

Instead I tell myself that the test results will be good for my heath, and the best is yet to come.

And instantly I begin to feel like a heavy load had been lifted.

I was free to see the good coming into my life.

I thanked my body for all it had done for me and would continue to do.

I was so tired, I turned over and went back to sleep

In an altered state of twilight sleep I saw my body grow stronger and more vibrant from my doctor's words. I was being healed. Thank you.

Imagination
The First Step
"Unconditional love is the most powerful stimulant of the immune system.
The truth is love heals.

"Miracles happen to exceptional patients every day – patients who have courage to love, courage to work with their doctors to participate in and influence their own recovery."

Dr Bernie Siegel.

How often has your body said no, and you went ahead, and things went wrong?

You fell in love against your better judgment, and then felt bad you couldn't make the relationship work.

These thoughts diminish your faith and health.

Imagine having a control tower in your mind that knows when to say yes and when to say no.

Trust yourself enough to hear, see, and feel messages from your control tower.

Imagination means allowing your creative mind to flow without interference from the logical fa

Everyone is born with six sense

You may have shut down because:

You couldn't handle the knowing

Your inner voice told not to trust yourself.

An event caused you to shut off your inner thinking.

Dan, believes in me and continues to give me the confidence to do public speaking, write books and private tutoring.

30

I knew that I had met my true love when Dan rescued me when I couldn't park my car correctly on a small side street in Chicago. I yelled up to the lady on the second landing of the apartment building and asked if there was a man who could help me park my car.

Down came a man with a beard in an Hawaiian shirt shirt saying, "I can help you. Where is your car?"

We walked together to my car and saw it sticking out in traffic. He moved my car easily in the speed of light and got my car out of harms way. He was my hero.

On our first date, we laughed and talked in a light shower of rain while walking three miles to a neighborhood restaurant for dinner. It was fun.

Dan's unconditional love gave me happiness and self-confidence.

Chapter 7

Protecting Your Inner Power

In an effort to help Penny see, we worked together on a past life and learned that she was a farmer, who had tried to rescue a friend, who had been put in prison for a crime he hadn't committed.

The military commander ordered the friend's three-year-old child's limbs to be tied to four horses, unless the man told him who helped him.

The farmer didn't cooperate and the commander shut a gun, and the four horses bolted and severed the child's limbs.

Penny shouted, "I can't look at this and ripped out her eyes."

Today Penny is blind, and still doesn't want to see evil things, but when she uses her inner power, she can give accurate ID descriptions and personality traits so the survivor will know she can speak to the dead.

She Brings closure to old wounds and finds lost items.

If I ask Penny why am I sick? Instantly she answers accurately.

I returned home from work one afternoon to hear Penny talking to someone in her bedroom. Curious I went to see who she was talking to and saw my dead mother's ghost laying on her bed. Terrified I told her to stop doing this.

As I left her bedroom, I heard Penny say, "My mommy's afraid. We have to talk quieter"

I told my mentor Paul Johnson, what I saw.

He said, "You have to stop being afraid of ghosts or you'll never become the great psychic you are meant to become."

He gave me private tutoring and started me on the path of spirit communication.

Today spirit tutoring is one of my favorite subjects.

I've written two books about how to connect with loved ones in spirit.

A 7 Step Guide to Spirit Communication
They Don't See What I See

Learn to trust your instincts
Be alert to what your body is telling you.
Eat when you're hungry.
Sleep when you're tired.
Change your thinking.
Make better decisions.

Working in the present time.
Letting go of limited beliefs.
Accepting yourself as you are.

The Three Steps to Medical Intuition are:

Locating the area in your body that is the darkest.

Discovering why and how the illness was planted.

Learning what you need to heal.

Chapter 8

The Miracle

Penny is an amazing psychic.

One day her friend Sheryl asked, "Penny, When will my child be born?"

Penny quickly got a calendar and opened it on a month and told Dana, her four-year-old daughter, and also a psychic, to feel each the page of each month. Just turn it and keep turning the pages till you feel heat.

Dana stopped on March and said, "This is the month and then Penny took her index finger and had her touch each day to which was warmest.

She stopped on the 25th. I told Sheryl, "We now have March 25th. Now Penny asked Dana what time of the day the baby will be born."

Dana quickly responded, "after breakfast." She was within fifteen minutes of the baby's birth time.

Penny asked Dana," If it is going to be a boy or a girl?"

Dana put her hand on Sheryl's tummy and said, "A girl." She was wrong because her ego got involved too much for her inner power to work correctly.

Adults can play this game too.

Soon after, four-year-old Dana took my migraine away by brushing her hand over my forehead. She clapped her hands and wiped them on her pants to rid the headache, so she wouldn't take the headache on herself. She said, "Grandma pain all gone. They took it away."

"Who took it away? I asked. She shrugged her shoulders and said nothing.

Stunned by the suddenness of how she rid my headache.

Everything came naturally to her, but she wasn't sure why or how.

Any age is the right time to connect with your inner power.

****

One morning. Dan found me unconscious in the bathroom. He called the Paramedics, who took me to the hospital immediately. The doctors didn't understand why I wasn't responding.

I spent fifteen days in the hospital for medical tests and different medicines to find what might give them more information. Nothing worked.

During my fifteen days of unknowing, Karri was at the hospital days, with Dan, who also stayed all night. They were my watch guards and protectors.

For fifteen days I lay in the hospital not knowing whom my husband or children were. Karri watched over me telling the medical staff of my reaction to noises. They didn't listen and when I went to get a medical test, they didn't sedate me and I had a seizure.

Karri was furious because they didn't believe her. After my seizure they listened to her.

Karri said, "There a story about people like you. The lights are on but there's nobody home.

You weren't home."

On my sixteenth day in the hospital I opened my eyes for the first time and saw a man with a stethoscope on his white coat, taking my pulse. After fifteen days of silence, I spoke my first words,

"I'm going to get well playing my piano."

The doctor smiled and nodded yes.

He didn't know about my musical background.

"He asked, "We'd like to send you to a nursing home for rehabilitation. Do you want to do this?"

I nodded yes and fell back to sleep.

The next morning I spoke again and asked Karri and Dan if the nursing home had a piano I could play?

They both smiled and said, "We'll look into it."

Dan asked, "Is there any special sheet music you want me to bring?"

"Yes. Anything written by Liszt or Chopin and Ave Maria.'

I still had problems remembering people, but music was different.

Karri taught me that music is always the last thing to go."

The following day I was taken in a wheelchair to the ambulance and driven to the nursing home.

I slept all the way, and didn't hear the siren or any noises.

I was taken to my new room and slept most of the day.

I was happy to be in a place with a piano I could play, but that's all I remembered.

It took me two more days of resting before I was wheeled to the piano room. Dan lifted me onto the piano bench and I looked at the sheet music Dan had brought, and began playing as if I was normal.

Karri and Dan were so happy to see that I still could play the piano.

I didn't want to stop, but a woman interrupted me asking,

"Who are you?"

"I'm a resident," I responded.

She smiled. "You play very well. Would you like to play for all our residents?"

To my surprise, I said, "Sure. When?"

She said, "Next Monday if you're able."

"How long do you want me to play the piano?"

"As long as you like, but usually twenty-five minutes or more," she answered.

"Fine and turned to Dan. Can you bring me more of my music?"

Dan smiled.

The rest of the week was a blur. I slept a lot and practiced the piano whenever I could.

People kept coming into the meeting room, when they heard me playing the piano to listen, to tell me how much they liked what they were hearing.

I asked Karri to introduce me, "Tell the residents that three weeks ago I didn't know you or anyone, and now I can play the piano.

I want them to have hope."

Karri smiled and said, "Of course I will."

I had no fear of playing the piano, which was unusual for me. I was always so critical of my mistakes. But not this time, I was too excited to have the opportunity to play the piano.

I played for thirty minutes and got tired and said, "I have to stop."

The residents asked me to play more. I played a short piece and said, "Thank you for all your kindness. Now I need to rest."

Someone brought my wheelchair and drove me back to my most welcome bedroom, where I slept the rest of the day and night.

During the next few months I was given physical and mental therapy and slowly, I began to recover much of what I had forgotten.

I was getting better, due to my piano playing and therapy.

I was slowly healing.

Chapter 9

Personal Tutoring

One afternoon a regular client was waiting in my office. Her aura was a dark haze, indicating she was in stress and needed my help badly.

She asked, "Ruth I'm beginning to lose a lot of my hair and I'm afraid I'll get bald.

"Do you have any ideas on how to stop my hair from falling out?"

I closed my eyes and entered a short meditation. Soon I said, "I don't feel you're going to lose all your hair, but you will attract what you think, so stop worrying about your hair loss. Don't rush trying to save your hair. ***Hurry restricts positive comments from getting through***.

"I'd like you to come to me once a week, for a few months. It'll be similar to the way I train people to use their inner power.

"Keep a journal with your thoughts, fears, dreams, and ideas and bring it with you to all our sessions.

"In the past we've talked about the men who come and go in your life. What's going on in your present day – to –day efforts?"

"Awful. I don't think I'm ever going to find the perfect partner."

"Why? I asked"

'She bowed her head and tears began to fall. "I'm getting too old, too fat, and now I'm going bald. What man is going to want me?"

"Let's start over. What type of man are you looking for?"

"I usually think about what I don't want. I don't want a cheater, a loser, or someone who will lie to me."

Ruth. "Have you attracted many men like that?"

Her eyes watered as she said, 'Yes."

"Let's try something. Imagine looking ahead five years from now. Your body is exactly what you've wished for, and your hair is full and shiny. You see a good-looking man walking towards you. He looks like everything you've ever wanted in a man. Now describe him."

Her face lit up as she spoke happily. "He's 6 foot 10" tall, strawberry wavy blond hair level with his ears, beautiful baby blue eyes, his eyelashes go and on. He's wearing a yellow button down shirt, the top three buttons are open and his sleeves are folded up to the elbow. He's got biceps like a weight lifter. What abs he's got! Wow! He's amazing!

"I wish he would turn around in those jeans. I wonder if his brain is as good looking as his body."

I stepped in and said, "Now I' want to ask you a totally different question. Why did your last serious relationship end?"

"I wasn't in a good frame of mind so I picked someone who was a drunk

"I choose men who came my way because I didn't think I could get anyone else. I had very low self-esteem,"

Caroline said she dabbed her eyes to stop the tears flowing from her eyes

I said, "You'll never find the right man, if you don't like yourself first."

"Next week I want you to bring a fairy tale of how you met a better man, where were you, what were you doing and what were you thinking/"

"I'll try." She kept hugging, like she didn't want to let go of me.

Caroline returned the following week she was beaming. "I had a great week pretending to be Cinderella. I met Prince Charming and he was everything I ever dreamt about. He was handsome, gracious, and generous. He even gave me a five-carat diamond ring. I had the best night's sleep ever.

"Then I woke up and realized it was only a dream, but it was so real. Do you think it could really happen?"

"Anything is possible, but for now, I'd like to ask you a few questions. What did you like the most about him?"

"He was nice, and so perfect."

"Where did you meet him in the dream?"

"We met on a park bench by a river. He saw me alone and asked if he could bring me a donut and coffee.

"Where do you usually meet men?"

"In bars."

"Why?"

"Usually it's easier to talk to them when they're more relaxed.

"What I don't understand is why a dream could make me so happy?"

"Do you remember the song, "When you wish upon a star, it makes no difference who you are."

"Dreams do come true. I know because that's how I met Dan, my perfect partner.

The dream is only the beginning. I'd like to interpret your dream with your permission."

"Sure, go ahead," she said smiling.

"You weren't at a known location or a bar, just a chance meeting. The man approached and offered you some food. Nice guy! You felt comfortable with him.

"You set this all in motion by thinking about what you really wanted.

"You attract what you think, and that's what you did in your dream."

Ruth said, "Years ago I remember sitting on a park bench near an ice cream vendor. A nice looking man on a bicycle sat down next to me and began talking, just like your prince. He offered to buy me an ice cream cone."

He said, "I'm looking for a woman who likes to rides bikes and enjoys boat rides, because I own a boat."

"I'm sorry but I'm happily married."

I wanted to ask him for name and phone number to give to my single friends but was too shy.

The first step of inner power is to believe that dreams can come true.

"Stop going to bars. Bars are a place for a simple drink with friends. Keep replaying the dream but ask for more information.

Ask your inner power to give you a place to meet men besides bars. You haven't had any luck finding your perfect partner in bars.

There's an old quote. Doing the same over and over, and expecting different results is insanity."

Change your mind change your life.

"There are many places to meet eligible men. I recommend becoming a volunteer at a hospital, charity group, or at a local grocery store.

"I always knock on watermelons to see if they are ripe enough to eat. One day a man asked me, "Why are you knocking on the watermelons?

I said, "If you knock and listen for the loudest echo, you'll find the ideal time to buy a watermelon. Try doing that the next time you go shopping."

He did and smiled when he heard a loud sound. He thanked me for my advice.

People enjoy learning new things.

Smiling is good way to introduce yourself.

The old adage, *"The way to a man's heart is through his stomach."*

Invite a man for a home cooked meal.

"Next week's homework is to volunteer and invite someone home to dinner. Doesn't have to be fancy meal, just a simple meal, you and your smile is enough.

"Keep a journal and bring it back next week."

Caroline returned with a troubled look. "I met a nice man but felt uncomfortable with him. He said he was a salesman of cars, but later he said he was a mechanic. Which was the truth? I wondered how many lies he'd told me?

'He said he didn't drink liquor, yet he had two cocktails while we had dinner.

"I was very uncomfortable. I didn't trust him."

'Very good!' I said. 'You're beginning to pay attention to what your body is trying to tell you. What were your physical symptoms when you felt he lied?"

She said, "I felt queasy and my forehead hurt like a headache was starting. I wanted to run away."

"The next time you get those feelings, pay attention to your body and think why you feel that way."

"In the meantime, get out more to meet new people like you. Have fun. We'll talk more next week."

Two weeks later Caroline said, "I think I've found Mr. Right, but I don't feel sure enough. I'm beginning to doubt me. What do you think?

R. "Tell me about this man. What is his name?"

Caroline said, "Jonathan. He's kind, polite, but sometimes I get the feeling that he won't be in my life long."

Ruth: "Is he sick?" Intuitively I knew the answer.

Caroline's eyes looked sad, "I think so. Sometimes he get white as a ghost when he's tired or in stressed."

Ruth: "Has he been to a doctor?"

Caroline: "Not that I know of. I've been afraid to say anything.

Three weeks later. Caroline came in sobbing: "Jonathan died last night from lung problems. He's been smoking for years. No wonder I didn't feel he'd be in my life too long."

"I don't want anyone smoking around me. Can I get lung problems from inhaling the smoke."

Ruth. "Yes. So trust your instincts more and do what you feel."

One month later Caroline returned. "I met two wonderful men and didn't have a lot of bad vibes, but when I found out that Drew was married and hadn't told me, I was devastated. Why didn't he tell me before we got involved?"

Ruth. "Why do you think he omitted telling you?"

Caroline. "He was afraid I'd break off with him. What do you think?"

Ruth. "I think you're right. Keep trusting your instincts."

Caroline. "I've met another man named Bob, whom I think is Mr. Right."

Ruth. "Start testing Bob. "What is he like around his family, friends, you? Does he treat everyone the same?"

Caroline. " I'm not sure".

Ruth. "How long has he been at his job?"

Caroline. "Just a few months."

Ruth. "Does he see your family?"

Caroline. "No. He'd rather not be with them. I love my family and wish he'd be more comfortable with them. They don't do anything to cause his reluctance. It makes me feel bad."

Ruth. "Always listen to what your body is feeling.

On our last session, Caroline reported, "My hair is growing back. I've lost sixty pounds and met my perfect partner. I don't have any more doubts. I'm happy."

Ruth. "Congratulations. You've been a good student. I'm proud of you. Keep listening to your inner power, and trusting what you hear."

A Growth Opportunity

A few weeks later, one of my friends gave me a set of six audiotapes to listen to, and tell him what I thought.

The tapes were about a valiant soldier trying to rescue a maiden in a castle. On the way an ugly devil confronted him and tried to stop him from reaching the castle, when he heard the maiden screaming for help.

Afraid he thought there was no way to fight the devil. He was stronger than me and could easily outrun me. I closed my eyes and began to pray for help.

How can I get away from him, I said to myself. I heard a masculine voice saying, "He can't handle love. It's the only thing that diminishes him. Tell him you love him."

I said it and when the devil shuttered and fell forward, I realized love was my best defense. I kept repeating I love you, and so does God over, and over as I watched the devil dissolve into a puddle of water, just like the wicked witch in the movie *The Wizard of Oz*. He was gone.

I was excited by this new revelation. I learned I could rid myself of fear by saying love thoughts. Amazing! I was proud of me.

"I won." I screeched. I told my friend what happened and he said, "Wow! I never thought to think love." That experience gave me a new way to control my fears. I thanked God for all his help. I was free at last to be happy.

A few weeks later, a tall, slim woman with black and white curly hair asked me about her abusive husband, hoping I could give her some advice. I wondered if the reason she was still with him, had to do with money.

I asked her, "Can you support yourself if you leave your husband?"

"No," she cried too loudly. "I don't have any business skills. That's why I haven't left him before. We have two children, my daughter is eight-years-old and my son is seven and autistic.

He needs a lot of therapy. I don't know if I can provide for my children and myself without the help of my husband's income."

Without her saying more, I knew intuitively her husband was insensitive and often verbally abused her. A sick man, I thought and wondered what I could say that could possibly help her.

I said to my client, "Let us sit quietly and pray to come up with a solution for a few minutes".

My client's aura lightened as she spoke first. "I don't know what this means, but I heard in my head talk to Ruth about love."

"That's it, I said," and with my eyes closed, told her what had happened to me the previous week while I listened to the audiotapes.

When I opened my eyes, my client's hazel eyes were wet and tears were streaming down her face.

She asked, "I don't love my husband any more. Do you think if I told my husband I loved him, it would help?

"I'm not sure," I said. "You could think love and mentally project your thoughts to him. That might work."

A week later she called and said, "I didn't think sending love messages could work, but it did. He's not saying nasty things to me, or the children lately. Bless you and thank you for all your input."

This time I was the one who was crying. "I'm so glad you're happier, but if you need me, just call."

I was busy seeing new clients, when an unfamiliar, sad looking man stopped by and said, "I talked with my friend and she recommended I contact you for help. We need to set up a session a few weeks off.

He was wearing a brown suit with a matching tie. He said, "I'm married to a woman who says, "If you don't let me hurt you, I will hurt your son."

"I love my son. She's hurt him before. He's only eight-years-old and small. I can't let her do that. I've been to the police, but they laughed at me."

They said, "You're six foot-two inches tall and she's only five foot six inches. Why can't you control her? We have nothing on the records that she beats you."

"I need to get a record on her beatings, but, when she's angry she's very strong and scary and starts to attack our son. My lawyer says the judge will never give me the child without my wife being on record for assaulting me. I don't know what to do. Can you tell me something good?"

"Yes, I said and told him the same story about the six tapes my friend gave me. Love is the magic elixir. Think love thoughts to your wife whenever she's going to hurt you and don't stop until she stops. Love thoughts diminish evil thoughts."

When I spoke in Las Vegas a few months later, a woman stood up and shouted, "I'm a police officer. I've been taught to train prostitutes how to change their thinking from fears to love thoughts, when the rapists want to hurt them.

It works, I've seen it work.""

Ruth. "Intuitively I've seen love thoughts reduce anger and hatred. You don't say the words aloud, just think it but look straight at your wife. Let me know what happens."

We talked more and he seemed happier. I prayed he would try sending love thoughts.

Four weeks later, he called me and said, "I tried sending love thoughts. It's hard but the more I did it, the less angry my wife was. I'm still afraid for my children, but life is better."

"I really dislike her and am afraid if I stop sending love thoughts, she'll get mean again. What can I do?"

Ruth, "Believe you can send her enough love to reduce her anger. Believe in God and believe in yourself. This woman is in your life for a reason. Think what you are learning living with her. Let me know what comes up."

He called me two months later and said, "Thank you. Life is much better now. I can't stop sending my wife love thoughts. It's made our marriage much more harmonious. Can I set up another session with you?"

"Of course. I can see you next Friday morning."

When I saw him again, he seemed happier, his aura was almost white.

He said, "My life has changed but I don't want to stay with my wife any longer. I am so confused. I thought we'd be together for all our lives. Tune into your inner power and tell me what you see."

"I closed my eyes and thought about him in the future. He was still married to the same woman and unhappy. He was still afraid. I got a message that he needed to have private tutoring to like him more. If he left her too soon, he would not find happiness.

I asked, "What did you want to be when you were a teenager?"

"Stunned, he blurted out, "Why are asking me that question? I've been thinking a lot about my future. I don't like what I'm doing now. I always wanted to be an artist. I love to paint, but haven't done it for years."

"I almost leaped out of my skin. You have a growth opportunity to change and be all that you ever wanted to become. Are you ready to move out of the past and into the future?"

He looked like a dear caught in a headlight. "I'd like to try but don't know how."

"Could you take art lessons part time?"

He smiled and said, "I don't see why not. I could still work and see my son. Yeah!.

Just thinking about art lessons makes me feel good."

"Always listen to what your body is trying to tell you. Right now you're happy just thinking about drawing again. If that feeling changes, ask yourself why? Then meditate on the answer and do what your mind tells you to do.

"Most of my answers come when I'm in twilight sleep, half awake and half asleep. Let me know if you need my help again."

Many months passed until one day he returned with a gift-wrapped painting. "Thank you for all your insights. I'm back to drawing and I have a gift for you."

He unwrapped the paper and showed me a painting of myself.

He said, "I thought you might like this. It's yours to keep."

"WOW! I said after unwrapping the paper. This painting is good. Thank you.

Ruth. "During my forty years of inner power I've worked with thousands of people about their lives, their children, and their lack of self-confidence."

"Trust your instincts and you won't go wrong."

I remember a slim woman asking for information about her husband. I don't know where he is or why he left. He's been gone for two years."

I suggested, "Sleep in the color pink (love) and try visualizing him returning home lovingly."

It took two years but he did return with love and lust in his heart," she said. "Now things have changed for the better. He shows me love and kindness. I am so grateful. Thank you for your help."

An older woman asked me about her sex life. "My husband doesn't want me any more. I've asked him to go for therapy, but he says no.

"Has he been cheating on me?"

Ruth. "I don't see him doing that, but he doesn't seem to have enough energy for sex. Have you noticed if he's been more tired than usual?"

. "Yes I have," she said. "He sleeps a lot and doesn't want to go out with our friends. I can't understand why. He always liked getting together with other people. Is it something I've done?"

"When I tune into his aura, I see him depressed. Have you noticed if he is?"

"Sometimes I think so. But he's do quiet, I'm not sure."

Ruth. "Can you talk to his doctor and tell him what hasn't been happening? You need medical advice.

Her aura shined a beautiful pink as she said, "Yes. I'll call him."

Smiling I said, "Good luck."

My daughter Penny just called. She said, "I just saw light for the first time. I'm so happy. Last night I kept saying I love me and so does God, for hours. I couldn't sleep, just kept saying love to myself. Today I see light."

I had been reading parts of this chapter to Penny and she tried the love thought suggestion. Amazing! I am delighted with this new turn of events.

****

A former client with a dark aura asked me, "Will I ever meet the right man to marry?"

I closed my eyes and asked my inner power to see her in one year. She was fifty pounds lighter and she had met Mr. Wonderful."

After I told her what I'd gotten, she smiled and said, "I'll see you in a year."

When I opened my office one morning a year later, she was waiting with a scowl on her face. I haven't met Mr. Wonderful and you said I would if I lost fifty pounds."

"Did you lose any weight?" I asked.

"No why should I?" You said I would meet him, and I thought I didn't have to do anything."

I told you the reading as it came to me, but you changed it. I'm not a magician. Try loosing the 50 pounds and then we'll talk."

"Okay," she said with her shoulders slumped forward, as she walked out of my office.

I was attending a meeting for mothers-to-be when one of the women in the audience asked, "Why does my older child cry whenever I hold him?"

I took her hand and felt her stress. I said, "Your body is so tense." And immediately saw her husband mentally abusing her.

Intuitively I knew he was a cruel, insensitive man who enjoyed frightening her.

Time changed and I saw her as a young girl who loved to sing, but when she married and grew older, she lost herself in negative thinking. I'm not good enough. People don't want to hear me sing.

These were words from her husband to be who lived next door to her family. She assumed these were her thoughts and believed them to be true. She kept hearing these words over and over until she stopped singing.

Now twenty years later she couldn't sing for fear of being ridiculed.

Then she heard the minister asking for a soprano for the choir. She raised her hand. The minister nodded for her to speak.

"I'm a soprano. Could I audition for the part?"

"You sure could," said the minister. "Our choir director is sitting at the piano. Tell her what you'd like to sing?"

"Ave Maria," she said smiling.

The pianist played the first chord and the woman began to sing like an angel. She wasn't thinking negative thoughts. She'd divorced her spouse a year ago and without him telling her how lousy she sang, she was delighted to sing at last.

There was a lot of applause as the audience stood up as one. "Yea! They yelled. She's good. Let's keep her."

The following Sunday she sang again happily.

Everyone in the congregation stood up together saying,

"We vote for her to be our new soprano."

Gratefully she sent kisses out to the people outstretching her arms as if to embrace them all.

Chapter 10

A Singles Party

Come One, Come All
Meet People who are interested in learning how to Use Their Inner Power to meet new people to Laugh and Talk.

Dress in the color that will help you more fully experience the evening of the party.

. . . .

RED	*Excitement*
Black	*Unknown*
Orange	*Care Taker*
Blue	*Higher Learning*
Pink	*Attract Love*
Purple	*Psychic Opening*
White	*Clear Seeing*
Brown	*Practical*
Gray	*Business*
Yellow	*Joy*
Green	*Growth Opportunity*

Jewelry to wear for the party:

Gold for Success
Silver for a Spiritual experience
Diamonds for clear seeing

The singles party event finally arrived. The women wore mostly pink and purple, and some wore diamonds. The men wore gray jackets with silver cuff links and ties A few men wore pink shirts.

Everyone was asked to meet five new people, say their own names and tell why they had come.

Immediately the room got lively and joyful while everyone began talking at once.

Ruth shouted, "Everyone Dose Doe to the person on your right corner. Stand still for a minute while gazing into each other's eyes. Notice what color the person's eyes are, and pay attention to what you feel.

Do you feel safe?

Are you uncomfortable?

Do you feel she/he likes you?

You're learning how to know more about a new person.

The more you know, the better you'll get at keeping your inner power.

"Wait a minute and walk to the partner on your left. Is his/her aura darkest on the left side or right side?

The left side represents the past,

while the right side represents present time.

The lighter the color, the more optimistic the person is, the darker color represents unresolved problems from the past.

Take a moment to just look into your new partner's eyes, and say what you imagine she or he does for a living."

Immediately everyone started to laugh. "Wait a few seconds to tell your partner what you got, and listen for his or her responses."

"It's important to take time trying this new technique to see how good you can do. If you get one hit, you'll feel great, two hits and you'll be ready to do more."

"The four levels of intuition are:

feelings tells us something is happening,"

Carl Jung said. "Thinking is next, that tells us what that thing is, the value of things.

Intuition is opening to possibilities, an ability to envision a single picture as the whole."

Ruth said, "When you have a hit, raise your hands and hug your partner."

People acted surprised by the amount of hands that were raised.

"When people are happy, they use their inner power more often."

Ruth asked loudly, "How many of you have the identical answers as your partner?

Six people raised their hands.

Ruth waited a few moments and asked. "Were your answers similar?"

The same six people raised their hands.

Ruth said, "It's always good to meet old friends."

Ruth's voice boomed, "Let's take the last thirty minutes walking and talking to more people, before we close this amazing evening."

As the evening grew late, people began to leave in twos, threes and singles, smiling and chatting. They kept thanking Ruth for the wonderful evening, and asking, "When can we have another singles party?"

"Watch for my next email," Ruth shouted as they left.

A few days later I saw two women sitting outside my office.

They said together, "Hi, we attended your single's event and need to talk to you. Do you have time to talk to us?"

"Sure, come on in."

Both women had short, wavy graying hair, and looked in their 60's. "Have a seat and tell me why you're here," Ruth asked.

The first women wore a silver pants suit with a pink blouse said, "We both attended your single's party and met each other there."

The other lady said, "Our husbands died the same day at different golf clubs, two years ago. Since then I've been very lonely and since I've met this lady, I feel like I've found an old friend. She's like a sister to me."

"My story is similar. I immediately felt I'd found my best friend when I met my new friend. We have the same interests, knitting, reading Danielle Steele's books, and writing. Now I'm wondering if we're getting too close. I'm not interested in a sex partner, just as a good friend.

I'm scared I might be gay?"

"No," I jumped in excited. "When people open their inner power, they begin to be more sensitive. The feelings you have are an extension of how much love you have to give or receive. Have you ever heard of soul mates?" Both women nodded yes.

"Have you ever heard of twin mates?"

Both women shook their heads no at the same time.

"That's when two people meet and instantly feel like old friends, have the same interests, and want to be together for more sharing.

"I think you're Twin Mates. It's as normal as the love that is shared between a new mother and a child, two siblings, or two good friends. It doesn't mean you're Lesbians, just loving friends without extra benefits.

Have you ever wanted to have sex with another female?"

"No," they both shouted.

"There's nothing wrong with sharing a place to live together, with your own bedrooms and living like friends together."

One lady said, "It feels right to me to."

"Me too," said the other woman.

"Thank you for listening."

A few weeks later an old client called for an appointment. We set it up and met the following week.

He began by telling me, "I'm in love with a woman of a different religion who I can't marry. I was raised by two parents, who believed that marrying people from the same faith, is the only way to find happiness. But this lady is wonderful and she makes me happy. I want to propose to her, but my past is getting in the way."

"Are your parents still alive?"

"No," he said, but I just couldn't go against them in life or in the hereafter."

"That's your choice, but have you tried to imagine life without her?"

"Yes," he said, "It only makes me feel sad. She's everything I want, but I just can't get past what my parents told me. I think, what if I marry her and we're not married in the church. I won't be happy."

"Have you talked to her about converting to your faith?"

"Yes," but she said she wouldn't. She doesn't understand why it matters so much at our age. I'm sixty-eight and she's sixty-five - A good age difference. We both still work and have busy, productive lives. What should I do?"

"If you can't resign yourself to living together without you or her changing your religion, then I think you have to move on. Have you thought about that?"

"Yes, but I don't want to date any other women. I am so confused."

"Try taking off some time from seeing one another and dating other women. See what happens. Maybe you'll find someone else that works for you."

He nodded sadly and left.

Four months later the same man returned to tell me, "Ruth I've been dating other women and no one makes me feel good. but I still felt guilty thinking of marrying out of my faith.

"Am I going to die a lonely old man alone"?

Ruth said, "That's up to you. I think you need to rethink about marrying the woman you really love.

"The first time I married," I said, "I married the wrong man, who was of the same faith as me. It never worked. We got divorced and after a few years I met my current husband, who is my perfect partner. He's also from my faith and it works well."

"I think it's time for you to stretch out to meet other women. Try other church groups, the internet, single groups, and try talking to women that you are attracted to. Perhaps this is going to be a new chapter in your life, one that will be far more adventurous and joyful than any in the past.

"My prayers and blessings are for you to find true happiness.

Bless you."

Chapter 11

Getting to Know You

The easiest way to meet someone is to notice a piece of clothing she or he is wearing, or an unusual tie, or a piece of jewelry and talk about why you like it.

I attended a class and saw a woman with a soft colored light blouse. I said, "Your blouse is unusual. Is the color teal?"

"I'm not sure," she said.

The woman sitting next to her said, "I think your blouse is green."

And we all began to talk.

Not rocket science, just an easy way to meet someone.

Volunteering in a hospital, nursing home, children's shelters, and other places that need volunteers, is another easy way to meet people.

Opening a door, picking up something a person dropped with his hands full, is always a good way to meet someone new.

Other easy ways to meet new people is to walk your child or a pet dog, to a park. Smile whenever you meet someone and talk about the weather, and notice what she's wearing.

"Where did you get that blouse? It's beautiful." Good opening.

Good manners make it easier for people to open up to you.

Opening a door when someone's hands are full, assisting people with a wheelchair to go first, and smile wide when you say hello.

Good morning, good day, have a wonderful time are all openings to say when meeting new people.

I like to attend talks at the library and discover what's new in medicine, theaters, and musical events. The most interesting things are happening everywhere. I've often discovered new friends.

One day I saw a young man in his 20s sitting at a table near the front door in a health food restaurant. When he'd see a lovely lady walk in by herself, he'd say,

"Are you dining alone? I am too. Would you like to join me?"

Brazen perhaps, but it worked.

People who need people are the luckiest people in the world.

Song lyric.

A friend was having trouble working the gas pump, and a man offered to help her. She offered him a cup of coffee for his trouble.

That was the beginning of a new friendship.

Chapter 12

Inner Power for Business

A client gave me fifty 3x5" cards to see if I could use my intuitive skills to tell him which leads were the best for him to follow up on..

When I know nothing about a subject, I close my eyes and ask my inner power to tell me what to do, and remain quiet until I get a message.

I held the fifty cards in my left palm (the hand for intuitive receiving), and waited for something to happen.

Within seconds I got the idea in my mind to touch each card for temperature shifts. The first card felt extra hot.

I turned the card over and read the name on it. The name made me shudder. "No, this is wrong," I thought.

"What's wrong? I asked myself. "My inner power said, "This person's name is wrong. He had written a false name. Why did he lie?"

I threw the card down away from me and picked up the next card. Thank goodness, my hand stopped hurting.

I asked my inner power why this card felt good. I heard the answer in my mind, "Trust yourself."

I turned the card over to read the name of the person. I felt calmer. "This is a hot lead." I said to my client.

He looked at the card and said happily, "I put this card in purposely to test you. This man has already said he's interested in purchasing land. Thanks for the confirmation."

I smiled gratefully. This was a new game I was trying out. It was nice to know I was on the right track.

I tried five more cards and didn't get any electrical impulses. I was beginning to wonder if I was stuck?

Then on the sixth card, my right forefinger began to shake. I turned the card over, read the name, and said, "Call this man first. He's a sure buyer."

My client's aura instantly changed from darkness to an emerald green color and as he smiled he said, "I know. He's one of my clients that has already put a deposit on one of my land purchases. Sorry for trying to trick you, but I had to be sure.

"I've spent so much time chasing dead leads. Forgive my doubts."

I said, "Actually you're helping me establish how this new system works."

I turned over another thirty cards and found six more positive cards.

Each time my client's head got bluer indicating he was using his higher intelligence to made notes on the cards to remind him later..

When I finished touching all the cards, I had three piles, hot, medium and cold. The hot pile was the shortest, but there were enough for him to begin using my system.

Later, he called and said, "You're so good. Each person had been waiting for me to call. I got three buyers on the first try. Fantastic!

"This is better than going to a casino and trying the slot machines, much cheaper, less time wasted.

He came often afterwards, and was always happy with good results.

I tried the same system when other people asked me about a new job opportunity.

One man said, "I have three job opportunities but I'm not sure which one to take. Can you give me any more insights on them?" He gave me three business cards to hold.

"I touched each card with my right forefinger and on the second card I got excited. "I like this one, but I see a red light in my mind. It's the best job, but I don't see you staying there long. Something's wrong with the company. Suggest you take a different opportunity."

He was disappointed. "I think this time I think you're wrong. I've already accepted the job and begin next week. I'll let you know what happens."

He called three months later apologizing. "You were right. The company went into bankruptcy and I lost my job. I reapplied to the second company you recommended and have a new job starting in a month. I'm sorry you were right, but glad I kept the second card in case."

A client asked if I could help her select a nanny for her three-year-old daughter. I asked, "Do you have a photo or letter from the nannies you are picking from?"

"Yes," she nodded and took a group of letters out of her purse.

She said, "One letter is from a young girl who lives in England, who wants to come to the United States." She handed me her letter.

I held the letter in my left hand palm and it felt nice. I was overly protective of children and wanted to be sure.

I opened the letter and read what the writer had written. It sounded good, but something kept me from letting go of the letter.

"What's wrong with this woman?" I asked my inner power.

Immediately I saw a vision of this nanny hitting my client's child. She was angry and wanted to hurt the small person. I didn't like this attribute and told my client.

She threw the letter into my wastebasket.

"Don't need this one," she said.

The minute she threw the letter into the trashcan,

I felt relieved and happy. "Good choice," I said.

I went through the other twelve letters and found one that pleased me, a young girl from Ireland. I held her letter and read it slowly while using my inner power to know more. "This one is good. She's reliable, honest and truly wants to help your daughter. This will be a good match."

She said as she put the letter into her handbag. "I'll let you know what happens. Thanks."

Six months later she returned with a glowing report, but said the nanny had gotten homesick and was returning home.

"Here's the latest letter I got from a friend of my former nanny. I like this one so much, I was afraid to show it to you for fear you'd say,

"She won't work out."

I took the letter and read it slowly. Suddenly I saw July fourth wireworks shooting out, I heard a band playing, hail hail the Gangs All Here.

I felt like I'd won the lottery, "No problem, she's a goodie. Don't worry, everything will work out fine".

We said goodbye and I didn't hear from my client for a long time. Then one day she returned to tell me that everything had turned out well.

Happiness flowed everywhere. "Thank you God."

Charter 13

A Journey for Love

"Love is not a final destination," says David Olmsted, "but an ongoing journey to explore and discover new things in our relationships."

Touch Power is fun, insightful and gives you the edge in dating.
Anyone can do it.
Increase your inner power quotient.

The purpose of Touch Power awareness is to sense how people touch you emotionally without the use of their hands or voice.
People watchers have been doing this game for years.
Some of the information you get is obvious, but not all.
Watching people is a non-involved way to increase your inner power.

I began using my Touch Power as a Standup Psychic doing ESP demonstrations, before hundreds of people.

Some people called me a combination of Dr. Ruth and Lilly Tomlin because I was funny, fast, and talked about sex.

In a forty-five minute demonstration I often ask for one or two individuals in the crowd, to join me on the platform.

This led me to utilizing my Touch Power to discover which individuals would agree to come before the audience.

I would look over the crowd until I felt heat over someone's head. When it happened I knew I had someone who would be a good subject on the platform.

My goal was to give her or him an accurate reading about their future that would be funny, but not scary or threatening.

One memorable message was for a woman in her eighties. I told her she'd find a great lover in six months, before the year was up.

She plunked down so hard in her chair that the noise reverberated throughout the room. "No way, I'm too old," she said.

A few minutes later, she stood up and said, "Will he be rich?"

The more I trusted my Touch Power with new people, the greater my accuracy became.

Consider how your feelings vary and change as you think about people you know, an ex-boyfriend, a good buddy, your boss or a neighbor.

Allow your mind to wander freely to reduce your thoughts to a single descriptive word for each individual.

Your ex-boyfriend is: unkind, harsh, bitter, spiteful, mean, sadistic, intense, creative.

You broke up with him because he was moody, troublesome, annoying, or upsetting.

Your boss is: affectionate, tender, likeable, delightful, often angry, indignant, resent, or vicious.

Your best friend is: happy, joyous, delightful, cheerful, contented, pleasing, imaginative, inventive, moody, and dramatic. Since she broke up with her fiancé she's sad, dejected, and disconsolate.

Intuition works instantly without the use of the intellectual mind. Write your instantaneous feelings for ten different strangers in a journal as quickly as you can list them, and discover how easily others, touched you in a non-physical way.

"Love is like a roller coaster. It takes you up to the top, and you have no idea what's on the other side. You can go with the flow, or jump off."

Penny Wagner"

My niece Dori, in her early 40's, was thin with short red curly hair, placed a creative personal ad in her local paper and got *one-hundred-thirty-five* responses.

Her ad launched her from the liquor industry to a media-advertising agency.

It wasn't until Dori spoke to the 134th man to contact her, that she knew intuitively he was her true love.

Here is a copy of her ad that she has given me permission to put in this book.
. . . .

SWF, 36, non-smoker/light drinker, educated, slender, attractive, athletic, honest, professional, is in search of a companion with similar attributes between 35 – 40, who would like to spend the winter keeping warm with a cuddly, affectionate companion, who enjoys laughing, playing, touching, and being held by a secure man.

Winter is closing in and I don't want to freeze.

Make that call!

*****

Touch Level 2.
Getting in touch with your gut reactions.

You can achieve a higher rate of dating good, honest and sincere men by paying attention to how your body reacts to them.

Listening to your gut instincts expands your intuition to understand and comprehend more about the people you meet.

Like an animal in the forest, pay attention to disquieting, perplexing, and anxiety vibrations.

When something doesn't feel right, stop whatever you're doing, look around and listen. Your mind is like a computer filming every emotional experience about the man your interested in.

Be alert to your feelings to know if the man you're talking to is *telling you the truth and is safe to go out with, or *if he will turn into a bad dream after a few dates.

In order to avoid drawing the wrong conclusion, ask yourself, "What's wrong with this person?

Why am I getting such bad feelings?"

Intuition works best when the hunch isn't thwarted by the intellectual mind.
. . . .

A young girl in her 30's raised her hand, "I thought I'd met my True Love. Now I wonder what I was thinking?

He's turned into a person I Don't like!

Why was I so blind?"

"Now you can try these two little tips to see if this person is right or do you want to go the other way?"

The young girl spoke again, "I lent my boyfriend of fourteen years $10,000 and he's stalling paying me back, and dragging his feet.

"He was supposed to invest it for met. Instead he's using it for his own purposes. Why didn't I see this deceitful side of him?"

Ruth answered, "You've been going with him for fourteen years and never saw this side of him?" Ruth laughed and so did everyone else in the room"

"The next time you touch his hand, check his mound of Venus, the fatty part, around his right thumb.

If it's hard - this is not a good time to get an honest answer.

The next time you ask for a payment, check his hand again and see if it is softer. Then ask for your money.

If his hand is still hard the next time, don't lend him any more money till he's paid your $10,000 loan back.

Negative reactions are more dramatic and easier to identify.

Visualize someone you loved in the past, who is no longer in your life. On a scale of 1 – 10, 10 being the worse, how strongly do you have one or more of the following feelings about him?

Confusion, perplexed, mystified, befuddled.

Some of your negative feelings can create a disease.

Where in your body do you feel these symptoms the most: stomach, head, lower, upper back, chest, shoulders, arms, feet.

Whenever you get a 10 on one of these symptoms, say no.

This is your body's way of telling you he isn't Mr. Right.

Good responses serve as a distraction from the negative feelings. Instead of a negative response, you may remember a beautiful memory of a blue sky, a mountain at sunset, a special kiss.

Think about someone you admire and like. How do you feel?

While dwelling on your friend, note from numbers one through ten.

The higher the number, the closer you're getting to know which partner is right for you.

Empathic people are individuals whose thoughts are often influenced by others, and because they are so open to others, their own wishes get pushed aside.

Have you ever had sex with someone, and the next day wish you hadn't? You just may be an empathic person!

Take a moment to ponder who's feelings you were picking up when you agreed to have sex with him? Could it be that you were taking on his wants, desires?

Psychics, therapists, and healers learn how to separate their feelings from the intuitive input they get from others to prevent burn out.

Often I ask attendees in a workshop to create two circles, an inner and outer one. To get a more accurate reading, it is important to stand directly in front of a partner.

At first they are asked to be totally silent for one minute, while they gaze into each other's eyes. After thirty seconds, they often begin smiling, followed by giggling before the full minute is up. Then they break out into loud, ear splitting laughter.

The purpose of this exercise is for people to stop worrying what to say or do with a new partner.

Then I suggest the inner circle move one person to the right, while the outer circle stays where they are.

This often causes some discomfort because they were comfortable were they were. Shortly after a few moves, the people begin to enjoy playing the game and meeting others.

The Hug – the ultimate Touch Power

Hugs can instantly change your thoughts.

In my original study group, I asked the attendees to hug two or more members and note how they felt.

The first hug I received felt great, and strong. The second person's hug was unpleasant. I discovered afterwards, she was angry with someone else.

Instead of shaking hands, or saying hi, New Age people like to use their Touch Power right away, believing three hugs a day, keeps the doctor away.

When you are hugged fully by an honest, true man, his energy will often make you feel solid, grounded, like finding your perfect place.

Whereas female energy, by a fine unselfish woman, might connect you to your spiritual level.

Loving hugs increase your energy while hugs from dishonest, unreliable people decrease your energy.

"More affectionate than a kiss, is a well done hug with someone you love." Carmen Miranda

Chapter 14

Take Charge of Your Life

"First comes thought, then organization of those thoughts into ideas and plans; than transformation of those plans into reality.

The beginning, as you will observe, is in your imagination."

Napoleon Hill

Have you ever noticed how strikingly beautiful a bride looks on her wedding day?

The men in the audience are aware of the bride's outer radiance as she walks down the white carpet to her future husband.

They are envious another man saw what they didn't see. They lost an opportunity. It may be too late for them, but not for you.

Try taking a year off from wanting, and date a lot different men to research what you truly need, not only what you want, but a man who will inspire you your inner radiance. Know that this is your year to blossom and to discover the real you.

Don't look at every man as a possible husband. Instead become the investigator, to discover what truly makes you happy, fulfilled and desired.

Keep a journal page on every man so you'll remember the good, the bad and the ugly.

When you first learned to drive, it was tough to remember all the basics. Blending your common sense with your power touch and inner thinking and knowing in this book is easier when you use them daily.

"Trust yourself. Create the kind of self that you will be happy to live with all your life.

Make the most of yourself by fanning your tiny, inner sparks of possibility into flames of achievement."

Foster C. McClellan

Example:
A man asks you to dance at a singles event.

Test 1. Touch power.
When he takes your hand, what do you sense: power, flabby, tenderness, or fear?

Test 2. Magic of Sound.
What does his voice remind you of: a happy encounter, or an angry episode?

Test 3. Aura seeing.
Look at his head. Do you see any darkness around his head, left side (present), right side (past)?

Each time you go on a date, begin using what you've read thus far, and discover which of your intuitive skills work best for you.

"Some people come into our lives and quickly go. Some people make the sky more beautiful to gaze upon. They stay in our lives for awhile, leaving footprints in our hearts, and we are never, ever the same."

Unknown.

"Only your connection with your own inner guidance, and your emotions are reliable in the end."
Christine Northrop

Author of Women's Bodies, Women's Wisdom.

Do you trust your inner guidance?

How often do you trust yourself when you are with someone?

Everyone has secrets. Some they know and others are lost in memory.

You may not know what a person's secret is, but you will often feel insecure about him or her, without knowing why.

Perhaps it's the way he/she moves his head, or drops his voice into a whisper that reminds you of someone, who hurt you in the past.

A secret of your own???

Speed judgment is making decisions that come from experience.

Awareness is the Key

When you are attracted to someone, be practical and use your common sense to stay balanced so you don't get hurt.

Trust is one of the most essential traits you must search for in the person that you want to spend the rest of your life with.

When someone lies, his aura will raise negative vibrations in your body, even if you don't know he's lying.

Truth makes you feel safe.

Hunches come unexpectedly through your imagination.

Example: you suddenly feel fear.

Say a prayer and give permission to your intuition to offer more insights; it might be that the man you're with isn't telling you the truth.

To Be or Not To Be Happy

There are no good men out there, either they are married or losers.

The woman's pouting mouth and angry face showed clearly her frustration.

A tall ravishing, beautiful African American woman was matched with a stunning, tiny young blond, blue eyed girl.

They were both creative writers in their spare time, while working full time as buyers for high priced women's clothing.

Another client said, "I felt the same about my former girlfriend until I saw her kissing another man in a restaurant after she'd promised she'd never cheated. Obviously she lied, but I believed her.

"I felt so betrayed and stupid for believing her. I'm confused because I still love her and want her back."

"I wasn't self confident enough to wait for a True Love. I took short cuts, not willing to know if they were telling the truth or not. How do I know when someone is telling the truth? I want to know how to see the truth or a lie?"

More hands rose up. One fifty year-old man with the stomach of a pregnant woman shouted, "Me too. I'm tired of being used as a checkbook.

"The women always say they'll pay it back, but they don't."

Chapter 15

Finding Mr. Right!

A woman with dark brown eyes and hair, with dark auras of black and gray, had a curvy overweight body, had on my suggestion decided to take a year off from wanting to find Mr. Right.

Divorced three times, she realized a need to change her thinking to have a long and lasting marriage.

After only thirty days, Sharma met Oslo, a

Swedish, tall, good-looking man, with long blond hair.

They had sex on their first night and often afterwards.

Sharma thought a year was too long to wait. They were married after two months and divorced one month later, after Sharma caught Oslo having sex with another woman in their bed.

"I should have known he was a liar and a cheater. All my husbands were the same as Oslo.

"Will I ever find Mr. Right," she moaned?

"Not if sex is the only way you judge men," I said bluntly!

"You don't have enough faith in yourself to research the men you sleep with.

"How did you feel after sex with Oslo?"

Sharma's shoulders slumped and her brown eyes watered up.

"He wasn't the best sex partner I ever had. He couldn't hold back from climaxing long enough for me to be satisfied."

Ruth, "I've learned that when a man has sex, he dumps his essence into the woman. If the substance is incompatible to her, she will feel used, unloved, and lonely.

"Before considering sex, use your touch power to test if you should have sex with a man.

"What else did you have in common," I wanted to know.

"Other than kissing and sex, not much," Sharma said softly.

"Dating is a two way partnership," I said. "You have to contribute to the relationship too."

I knew it was time to tell her the truth.

"You're an intelligent woman, the CEO of a large advertising agency, who can sell and manage employees. You have a lot to offer a man.

"Don't sell yourself short. Now start over, take your time to find Mr. Right, and don't have sex until you've had enough time to know you've met your true love."

"The greatest happiness of life is the conviction that we are loved, loved for ourselves, or rather loved in spite of ourselves."

Victor Hugo

Two strangers at a party are suddenly aware of one another. They feel a magnetic attraction that compels them to gaze into each other's eyes, from across a room filled with people. They don't see anyone else, only one another.

They walk towards the other, never loosing eye contact. They begin to talk and time passes, as each finds the other fascinating, not wanting the moment to end.

The man thinks, "This is the woman I have been searching for."

The woman thinks, "Can this be real? Is this the man I have been waiting for?"

They question their hearts, but the attraction is so strong, that they block all other thoughts, but their immediate desire for one another.

"Love they ponder! Is this what love really feels like?"

Another part of their minds searches for another answer.

Her ex-husband has cruelly beaten Mary, the woman in our story.

She grew up in a family that was always on the edge of violence.

An alcoholic mother, a father who wanted to rule his home like a conquering warrior, and a severely emotionally disturbed sister.

She had been the one who had to diminish her own desires. She grew up with many secrets that she could not reveal.

Never learning how to help herself, she married a man just like her father, only instead of verbal abuse; he broke her arm after twisting it beyond its limits. Fortunately for Mary, he had found another victim and divorced her.

Mary has almost died from lack of love. It seemed her life was filled with people like her family, and for a long time, she didn't try to save herself.

John had grown up in a home, where people didn't talk or share their feelings. Both parents didn't know how to touch or express themselves. He grew up always wanting love, but not knowing how to get it.

John married a woman just like his mother. She was distant, cold and refused any intimacy.

After ten years of rejection, he had a brief affair with a woman, whose name he couldn't even remember.

He confessed his affair to his wife, and she divorced him immediately, taking every cent he had earned.

John withdrew even further into himself and almost committed suicide.

Now Mary and John meet in a crowded room and ask, "Is this love?"

How can these two sensitive individuals get beyond their pasts and find the love they want?

They went to different therapists and learned to break old patterns, get past their fears of being hurt again, and the healing began. They were not bad people, just programmed wrong.

They learned to have a plan for love, write a script and now know how to meet their True Love.

Get past your illusions and into reality. It is far better to see the truth and work with it, then deny true happiness because you can't see getting what you deserve.

Put down every single thought about your ideal partner, age, gender, physical appearance, occupation, academic background, religion, skin color, hobbies, interests, family connections, married/single or never been married, and other traits you are comfortable with.

Then write down all the same information about yourself and be brutally honest. Don't lie to yourself.

This is where you begin the rest of your life.

Are you ready to meet this person? Can you keep up with him/her? What have you done to help you find true happiness with a man?

Timing is critical. If you meet your ideal partner and can only hyperventilate, chances are you will not make a good impression unless he is a paramedic. He might be the type who enjoys being needed and you are both off to a good start.

The next step is to have a plan, a script.

How will you meet your ideal partner?

Waiting for someone to find you is probably the least likely way.

I have met many individuals who wanted to meet a wonderful person, sitting at home thinking about it.

These people are afraid to be hurt, and give themselves all types of excuses not to go out.

Einstein said, "Imagination is more important than knowledge."

Be creative. You want to find a certain kind of person. Then imagine where such a person could be found.

Not all marriages were created at a singles dance.

You can meet your special person doing laundry, buying produce, getting a book at the library, in church, at a lecture or night school class, personal ads, through a friend, bowling, skiing, walking, bird watching, etc.

The important lesson here is to get beyond your limitations, past failures and discover your gold mine.

You are a walking library of knowledge. Know what you like to do and what you want out of life. Create that same life in your mind to find your ideal partner.

Begin to create how you will meet your true love, when, where and how. Become your own psychic and see your future unfolding and bring happiness to you instead of pushing away love opportunities. You will magnetically draw them to you.

"There is no fear in love, but perfect love cast out fear."

John. IV.16.

It is not blindness that your partner will be, but filled with understanding, support and kindness that will become a way of life for both of you.

Living with a perfect mate requires your growth, your ability to go beyond yesterday's knowledge. Without growth, there will be stagnation and ultimately death.

Imagine watching the same reruns for days, months, and years. To keep your life from being a rerun, add chapters and events. If, you have the ideal partner, s/he will do the same for you. bring an idea, a story to light up your lives.

"Good luck is a lazy man's estimate of a worker's success."

Anonymous.

Chapter 16

The Soul Mate Test

A client asked, "Am I getting a psychic hunch or being overly concerned about my relationship with my future wife?"

I looked puzzled. "I'm not following you. Please explain."

The client continued. "I'm not sure how to put my feelings into words. I love my future wife. She is great, but I want to run away every time I think about marrying her."

"Now I can help you. What three things annoy you most about her?"

"She's perfect." He said. "I can't think of anything."

Ruth: "If you can't find three things wrong with her, you're not looking. You just want to pretend everything is fine."

"Well, she taps her nails on the table after she eats, and is always on the phone."

Ruth: Think up another flaw, even thought it isn't as significant."

The client says, "She tells her sister everything about us, whether it's private or not."

"Good! Now close your eyes and imagine living with these flaws for 20 years.

A frown appeared on his face. "I can live with the tapping. I can even accept her being on the phone all the time, but if she's going to tell her sister all our private conversations, I don't think I can trust her."

Ruth: "Have you told her how much her telling all your private secrets to her sister irritates you?"

He shook his head no.

Ruth: "Then talk to her. Tell her what bothers you. It's my intuitive feeling that she'll stop talking about your personal lives to her sister, and be more sensitive to you."

"Reflect on answers to the following questions about your woman?"

What are her religious beliefs?

How does she act with her family?

Does she put on airs with her friends?

How many children does she want to have?

What are her interests?

Is she open to change?

Does she spend more money than she earns?

If the answers to these questions agree with your lifestyle, you can be confident that Anne is the right woman for you.

Now ask if you could pass such an inspection if she were to check you out?"

He gulped, "I don't think so."

Then his aura changed to a bright yellow as he smiled. He was getting answers to some of the questions he'd been thinking about.

"My girl acts the same loving way with her family and friends. She loves her job and her boss wants to make her a partner.

She is a little frugal, but so am I.

We share a lot of the same interests.

The rest I'll have to think about.

Then he slapped his hand on his thigh as he beamed and said,

"She's a great gal. She's everything I want.

20 years I could do easily.

Soul Mates don't just walk away.

What three faults can you find in your partner?

Can you live with them for 20 years?

Can these faults be changed?

If you find more than three faults, you might want to rethink this relationship.

Chapter 17

The Room of the Intuitive Future

The circular room had mirrored walls, a silver tiled floor littered with colored pillows, and laser beams of rainbow colors shooting into the center, while whale and seagull sounds emanated from the speakers.

Two computers and two rainbow colored Plexiglas chairs were positioned opposite each other, at tables throughout the room.

The room became electrified as many people entered the room.

"Welcome!" Ruth said, "Please sit on a pillow of your color choice. The future is going to be here faster than the speed of light. Everything will be accelerated and you won't always have the time to check out the facts before making a decision."

"Today we're going to have a training session to help you know instantly when to trust what someone tells you and when not to.

Look at the people in the circle. Each of you will experience a different energy from each person. You can feel the energy in your body, or see an aura color through your sixth sense.

"What do you see in the woman's aura across from you?" I asked.

"I'm not sure if I'm seeing correctly," one man answered, "but it looks thin and dark."

"How does her aura feel to you," I asked?

"I'm not sure," the man said as he looked away. He didn't want to say how awful she made him feel, as he began to scratch. His body was itching all over.

The woman's face turned red as she said, "You're not comfortable looking at my aura, are you?"

Embarrassed, the man stammered, "I think you're pretty, but unhappy. I've been in other relationships that made me feel this way.

I don't want that feeling any more. I'm sorry. I don't know what else to say."

Suddenly the woman wiped her eyes, understanding instantly why men weren't attracted to her. They were turned off by her negative energy.

She hadn't realized how her aura reflected her feelings and how other people were affected by it.

Now at last, she knew what to do. She was going to think positively so her aura would radiate love, not depression. She vowed to herself, she would try not to be depressed as much.

Ruth said, "Now look at your partner. What do you sense?"

The woman's aura lightened to white as she was relieved to see a white aura around her partner's head. She didn't want to say bad things about anyone. "He makes me happy. I feel like hugging him."

In unison, the group said, "Go ahead. Trust your instincts.

Both people jumped up quickly, their pillows flying as they met in the center of the room.

They hugged hard and laughed, and everyone laughed with them.

"When the right connection happens, it's contagious. Everyone feels good, but this doesn't mean they're soul mates, just a good connection has been created."

The new spirit leader, Ishmael said, "Pick a partner and go to one of the tables. The computers are already set up for you. Type in your name, and date.

"Look at your partner's aura and type in which side is brighter; the left (the factual side) or the right (the creative side.)

"I'm going to ask you five questions you couldn't possible answer from just your looking at your partner. You're going to rely totally on your intuition."

On man looked bewildered. "I don't understand how to do this?"

Ishmael said, "The answers will come if you just relax and trust yourself."

The first man nodded, but still looked baffled.

"Look at your partner.

Question one. Under the age of five, did s/he have a pet? Type in your response."

To the man's surprise, he knew the answer. His partner had a pet snake named Skeezer, when she was four.

Question two. Where was your partner born? In this city, state, country, or in another part of the world? Type in your answer."

The woman was born in Russia. She wondered if her partner would pick it up?

Question three.

"Which place in the family order did your partner fall? For example, were you the first born, second, last, or are you an only child?

Questiion four.

"What is your partner's favorite color?"

"The fifth and final question is where would your partner like to live?

After you've typed in all your answers, let your partner check your accuracy."

The first woman screamed, "How did you come up with the name Skeezer? I had a snake with that name. How did you know?"

He shrugged his shoulders. "I haven't got a clue. I heard the answer and wrote it down, figuring I was way off. I'm more surprised than you."

The man didn't know that his partner was born in Russia, but he did guess that she wasn't born in the United States. She had no accent that would give away where she was born.

All the students were surprised at their accuracy.

The woman got four out of five; some had three or four answers correctly.

Ishmael explained. "There are no accidents. You and your partners have much in common.

"For the next few minutes, compare our likes and dislikes and see how many similarities you both share. Talk, listen and learn."

Five minutes later, Ishmael asked the group, "Raise your fingers to indicate how many similarities, five fingers, both hands fingers spread apart indicates ten similarities, then you can close your hands and hold them back up if you had more than ten similarities."

There were fifty people in the room holding up their fingers often showing more than five – five similarities, ten fingers up, ten similarities, and more."

Chapter 18

Understanding is the Greatest Gift

"To effectively communicate, we must realize that we are all different in the way we perceive the world, and use this understanding as a guide to our communication with others."

Tony Robbins.

Many years ago I read a book, that I cannot remember the title of, that was about two earths, one in present time and the other in the future.

The author wrote that the future Earth would let you replay your life to correct your mistakes.

I've written this book to help individuals to find their Soul mates to love, honor and cherish.

One woman with a bright red aura showing her excitement as she shot her hand up. "We found 16 similarities. My partner and I are the youngest of three, like the same ice cream, bubble gum, TV shows, colors, music, movies, rainstorms, rainbows, meditation, big fluffy pillows, read the same books, live in the same town, grew up in the same city, had mutual friends as children, don't like liars, and we both play the piano.

"We discovered we were both born in the same hospital, the same day within an hour of one another.

Who knows our bassinets may have touched!"

"Elena, did you feel something special with Steve?"

"Yes! It's been a long time since I've been close to a man. Steve made me feel special. He didn't do anything. I don't get it."

Her aura darkened.

"You feel good when you stop judging yourself, enough to trust you. Look at him. Who does he remind you of?"

Another woman began crying, "He doesn't look like my uncle Roger, but he smiles like him. Roger was my favorite relative. He always knew the right things to say or do.

"He's dead now and I miss him.

The man next to her put his arms around her shoulders and her aura lightened.

Ishmael asked him, "What are you feeling about all this?"

"Bewildered and stunned by her accuracy. We have so much in common. It's creepy."

Ishmael said, "The first time you get the right answers intuitively, it can be scary, but the more you do it, the more you'll be able to accept it. And the more you're right, the more you'll feel good.

"Now change partners and do the same exercise again."

This time there was no hesitation from the attendees. Everyone seemed happy and willing to repeat the lesson.

After five minutes Ishmael said, "Exchange your answers and check out your similarities."

This time most of the participants got four out of five answers correct and had at least ten similarities.

Ruth said that many of the people she loved who had passed over had joined their group, loving the loving energy.

Ishmael beamed as he said, "You're all good. This is one of the best groups we've ever had.

"Try this exercise on everyone you can. Notice any resistance.

The more accuracy you have, the more open you are to a better understanding.

"Understanding is the greatest gift you can give someone. You can use this to have better relationships. You can use this training to envision and recognize your soulmate when you meet.

"I want to congratulate all of you for having completed our course. I hope you will use all the intuitive tools to find your soul mates.

'Keep tuning in and meditating."

Everyone stood and applauded, and then hugged other members.

"Beginning today, treat everyone you meet as if they were going to be dead by midnight. Extend to them all the care and kindness and understanding you can muster, and do it with no thought of any reward. You life will never be the same again."

Og Mandino

**To The Amazing People In My
life Who Have helped me.**

Dan
  Husband of 43 years
  Advisor, best friend
  Editor

Karri:
  Oldest daughter
  Masters degree in nursing
  Psychology

Penny:
  Youngest daughter
  Advanced Ghost communicator, Psychic
  medium1331

Grandaughters:
  Dana, practicing psychic,
  Chris, loving healer, Mother of 2 sons,
  Christoper and Alex.

Ruth Berger
  Author of six how to books
  Owner of Paranormal center, book store,
  workshop, readings,
  Teacher, Coach, Trainer

Awareness: I saw a gypsy would often pinch her child's bottom when a tourist would walk byl